A NOTE TO PARENTS ABOUT BEING DESTRUCTIVE

"But it was an accident!" This is the excuse most children provide for being destructive. However, most destruction is not accidental. In addition, there are very few no-fault accidents. Being destructive is usually a result of willful intent or careless, disrespectful behavior. In both cases, the negative feelings and attitudes that lead one to destroy something are often as bad as the destruction itself.

Helping your child avoid destructive attitudes and behavior begins with teaching him or her to be respectful.

If a toddler were placed among a collection of everyday toys and price-less antiques, he or she would no doubt treat the toys and antiques equally. This is because young children know nothing about antiques and therefore have no respect for them. Teaching your child to be respectful begins with helping him or her understand the purpose and thus the importance of every person, place, and object that surrounds him or her.

Discussing this book with your child will help him or her become a less destructive and more respectful individual.

This book belongs to:

_____

Published by Scholastic Inc.
90 Old Sherman Turnpike, Danbury, CT 06816.

SCHOLASTIC and associated logos are trademarks and/or
registered trademarks of Scholastic Inc.

ISBN 0-7172-8596-0

First Scholastic Printing, October 2005

A Book About
Being Destructive

by **Joy Berry**

SCHOLASTIC INC.

New York   Toronto   London   Auckland   Sydney
Mexico City   New Delhi   Hong Kong   Buenos Aires

This book is about Lennie.

Reading about Lennie can help you understand and deal with **being destructive.**

You are being destructive when you:
- break something,
- ruin something, or
- make a mess.

You are being destructive when you *break something*. If you break other people's things, try to fix them. If you cannot fix them yourself, ask for help.

You are being destructive when you *ruin something.* If you ruin other people's things, try to replace them.

You are being destructive when you *make a mess*. If you make a mess, clean it up.

Wanting to know what something is and how it works might cause you to be destructive. You might handle something to learn more about it. You might ruin it if you do not know how to handle it in the right way.

Avoid being destructive. Do this instead:
- Talk to someone. Find out what things are and how they work before you handle them.

Having an accident might cause you to be destructive.

Avoid being destructive. Do these things instead:
- Pay attention to what you are doing.
- Handle things carefully.
- Move cautiously when you are around things that can be broken easily.

Not caring about something might cause you to be destructive.

Avoid being destructive. Do these things instead:
- Try to understand that things around you are important.
- Try to take care of them.

Being angry or frustrated might cause you to be destructive. You might abuse things when you are angry or frustrated.

Avoid being destructive. Do this instead:
- Calm down before you handle anything that could be broken or ruined.

Avoid being destructive. Do this instead:

- Stay out of places you have been told to stay out of. There might be things in those places that could be broken or ruined.

Avoid being destructive. Do this instead:

- Do not touch things you are not supposed to touch. They might be things that could be broken or ruined.

You might need to be punished if you *disobey* and are destructive. The punishment should help you learn that you must *obey* when you are asked to leave something alone.

You might need to be punished if you are destructive because you *do not care.* The punishment should help you learn that you need to *care* about the things around you.

You might need to be punished if you *choose* to be destructive. The punishment should help you learn that you should not be destructive *on purpose.*

Being destructive hurts yourself and the people around you. That is why you should not be destructive.